Social Constructivism & Christianity

Second Edition

Stephen W. Jones

I Am Intercultural

Social Constructivism & Christianity
Copyright © 2018 Stephen W. Jones

This title is also available as an ebook.
Visit: www.iamintercultural.com

ISBN 978-1-940105-72-7

I AM Intercultural
A division of Excegent Communication, LLC
Watertown, MN
www.excegent.com

Because of the dynamic nature of the internet, any web addresses or links contained in this book may have changed since publication and may no longer be valid.

All rights reserved. No part of this publication may be reproduced, stored in a retrieval system, or transmitted, in any form or by any means, electronic, mechanical, photocopying, recording, or otherwise, without the prior written permission of the Publisher.

Cover design: Andre R. Fonseca
Interior design: Andre R. Fonseca

CONTENT

Dedication 5
Acknowledgements 6
Forward to the 2016 Edition 7
Forward to the 2018 Edition 10

Chapter One: Introduction 11
    What this booklet attempts to accomplish 13
    The journey ahead 14

Chapter Two: Constructivism 17
    Culture 18
    Radical Constructivism 19
    Social Constructivism 21
    Cybernetic Constructivism 23
    A Summary of Constructivism 23
    Assigning Values and the Trap of Reification .. 26
    Implications 27
    Ontological Options 27
    Relativism 28
    Power and Society 29
    The Necessity of Subjectivity 29

Chapter Three: Common Christian Problems with Constructivism. 35
    Absolute Truth 36
    Morality 38
    Turning Toward Synthesis 39

Chapter Four: Relational Truth and Rational Truth 43
    How this Approach Connects to the Previous Chapters 44

Ways of Knowing:
An Oversimplified Introduction 45
Rational Knowing 47
Relational Knowing 48
Constructivism and Knowing 50
Fundamental Truth 51
Knowing Truth Differently 52
Relational 52
Rational 53
Implications 53
The Absolutist and Moralist and Truth 54
Where Do We Go from Here? 56

Conclusion 61

Resources 63

Dedication

This small book is dedicated to the memory of my mother, Susan Jones. I cherish the many years of love and support that you gave to our family, both when we were children and as adults. I am so grateful for the ways that you sought to engage us in the cultures of the places we lived. I am also grateful for the influence of the steady stream of international students that were in our house as you taught English. It was not until I was an adult that I realized what a privilege it was to grow up in a house where there were people present from around the world several days every week.

Thank you for the example you set in serving others - both those like you and those who were different from you.

I miss our long conversations about faith, life, culture, family, ideas and possibilities, and I have a feeling that we would have enjoyed talking about this little book. We miss you but we are so grateful for the life you lived so well.

Stephen W. Jones
August, 2015

Acknowledgements

Josiah Enns and Michial Farmer, thank you for your feedback on this short book. I appreciate your critical thinking and encouragement.

Darin Mather, thank you for your involved feedback and your contributions to the text, especially in chapters two and three. I enjoyed interacting with you over this material.

All three of you, it is a pleasure to work with you.

I am also grateful to Jennie. It is a privilege to do life together in our "growing and becoming."

Forward to the 2016 Edition

The importance of the perspective advocated by this book is testified to on a daily basis as I reflect on the news from around the world. Daily I see reminders of the all-too-common inability of people to actually understand each other. The powerful effects that come from a need for affirmations of constructed identities have, in just over the last month, been displayed in events ranging from the slayings at the Pulse in Orlando to the bombings in Istanbul and Baghdad, the shootings in Bangladesh, and the defensive nationalism that was part of the story of the Brexit, the UK's referendum on departing the European Union, to say nothing of the tumultuous 2016 US presidential contest.

This book does not seek to explain those events. Instead, this is an attempt to unlock the tool of constructivist thinking (more accurately constructivist epistemology) for those Christians who have been reluctant or unable to access it. As Christian thinkers find themselves in possession of a different kind of tool for explaining the world, it is my conviction that they will be better able to assess and interact with the world around them.

When I wrote this small book a year ago, I had hoped that by this point, a year later, that I would have found a book that could replace this one. Alas, I have not. I have found many excellent works that address the themes present here indirectly, but none which do so with the intentional focus on constructivism or with its importance for the understanding of intercultural communication, specifically from the perspective of the Christ-follower. No doubt, the epistemological frame of constructivism is itself a rather Western undertaking, with Giambattista Vico (ca. 1710) among the earliest of constructivists[1] and much of the recent development of constructivism happening in the West.[2] I had also not realized, a year ago, quite how many types of constructivism there are.

The constructivism advocated by this book is certainly social,[3] but it is also radical[4] and cybernetic[5], following the lead of Bennett.[6] Reflecting on Riegler,[7] it seems likely that there are those who will claim that the approach advocated in this book is overly representational and insufficiently agnostic about reality. Indeed, I had certain commitments about the nature of reality before I wrote the book.

However, the intent of this book is to suggest that constructivism is not de facto and necessarily opposed to the theistic arguments of this book. Certainly, other constructivists may come to very different conclusions than those that I advocate for.

If the forward thus far has seemed to be gibberish, it is my hope that you will find that by beginning with the introduction it is much more approachable.

S.W. Jones
July 2016

Minnesota

---

[1] Glasersfeld, "An Introduction to Radical Constructivism."

[2] For example, consider the Constructivist Foundations journal, which is perhaps the premier journal of constructivism today, and which is hosted by the University of Vienna.

[3] Berger and Luckmann, The Social Construction of Reality.

[4] Glasersfeld, "An Introduction to Radical Constructivism"; Glasersfeld, "Why People Dislike Radical Constructivism."

[5] Foerster, "On Constructing a Reality'; Glasersfeld, "Knowledge for Sustainable Development."

[6] Bennett, Basic Concepts of Intercultural Communication, 1998; Bennett, Basic Concepts of Intercultural Communication, 2013.

[7] Riegler, "Editorial. The Constructivist Challenge."

Forward to the 2018 Edition

In 2016 I noted that the rapid shifts in the socially constructed world indicated the need for a deeper understanding of the themes presented in this book. The intervening years can hardly be said to have lessened that need. As social constructs - in the forms of norms and institutions - are actively contested in front of us on a daily basis, it is perhaps a good moment to consider how it is that we know what we know, and what truth and ethics look like in light of how and what we know.

I have lengthened some of the chapters and eliminated others so as to provide a more concentrated focus on the issues at hand. I hope the reader finds this sharpened focus useful.

S.W. Jones
July 2018

Minnesota

Chapter One
Introduction

The complex world that has emerged in the first decades of the second millennia have left little reason to suspect that humanity has finally discovered how to live peaceably together.

Unfortunately, many of the efforts that have been made to build peace across divisions of race, ethnicity, nationality, and religion, have done little to help. A few years ago, it was appropriate to suggest that many people are now suspicious of efforts toward multiculturalism or racial sensitivity.[8] Today there is sometimes even open hostility to such ideas.

I believe that a portion of that suspicion is well-placed. I myself have participated in conferences and workshops where the mantra of tolerance seems to be far too feeble to answer the deepest questions of the day.

---

[8] Meer, Modood, and Zapata-Barrero, Multiculturalism and Interculturalism.

However, rejection of peaceably resolving differences is not necessary. I suggest that a much more useful approach is an intercultural approach that acknowledges the significant differences that remain present even when the shared humanity of people from different groups is fully acknowledged and embraced.

The pages that follow are an attempt to briefly lay the foundation for that approach, one that recognizes both shared humanity and fundamental differences across cultural groups. The approach taken here is based in constructivism - a word that is unfamiliar to many, but which also has negative connotations for some. Nonetheless, I believe it is an approach that is useful not only for liberal scholars, but also for followers of Jesus who may find themselves at any number of perspectives along a conservative-liberal spectrum. One of the great things, as well as one of the dangers, of constructivism, is that the end is not foreordained. It is not a teleological system or approach. Rather the opposite, it is a perspective which pushes us to find the beginnings of our knowledge rather than to presuppose the ends of it. But, perhaps we are getting ahead of ourselves. Let me first let you know what I do not intend to accomplish, and then what I hope to do.

This short guide is not intended to be a thorough nor irrefutable treatment of constructivism, whether social, radical, or cybernetic. Neither is it intended to be an apologetic for or against any form of Christianity or any other religion. There are intentional limitations in the treatment of theological concepts, and if at any point this work varies from an orthodox[9] view of God or truth then the error is likely in this work.

What this booklet attempts to accomplish

Despite these limitations I think I have found something about which it is both worthwhile and appropriate to write, and all the more as postmodernity intensifies into post-postmodernity (described by some as the intensification of everything).

As a student of intercultural and international relations I have come to rely on the concept of constructivism, in its various forms, as a very useful way to understand the world. However, I have, as a follower of Jesus, noticed that some of my fellow Christians seem hesitant to allow for constructivism in their treatment of culture or cultures. Whether their hesitance is intentional or is borne of a lack of familiarity with the approach, this lack seems to unnecessarily limit the usefulness of their work.

So, the goal of this brief work is to illustrate in fairly straightforward language a way in which Christians can develop an approach to *knowing* that brings together important insights from the constructivist approach with a Biblical worldview and what is ultimately a theologically[10] sound and Christocentric understanding of the world.

---

[9] Of course, the question of who determines orthodoxy and theological soundness is an important one."

[10] See note 9.

The journey ahead

So that the reader may better comprehend the intended flow of the argument, I have briefly outlined the remaining chapters of this book.

Chapter Two includes a short sketch of constructivism, with a brief consideration of reification and four implications of constructivism.

Chapter Three highlights two main objections that some Christians have with constructivism.

Chapter Four looks to resolve the tension between Chapters Two and Three through the suggestion of a way forward. This chapter not only accounts for these primary issues but furthermore looks to find truth that encompasses and surpasses two major epistemological frameworks in the search for that resolution.

Finally, a brief list of resources is presented, which the reader may find useful in further exploration of this topic.

As previously stated, this booklet is not intended to be comprehensive. It may be that this work will, at some future point, be elaborated further. For now, it is my hope that this small volume will be of some assistance to those who encounter it.

Introduction

Chapter Two
Constructivism[11]

I first came into contact with constructivism under the tutelage of Milton Bennett, who viewed the approach as foundational to intercultural competence. This was a surprise to me, as I had made my way through my undergraduate intercultural studies major without ever encountering the concept of constructivism. Although I was familiar with many of the intercultural frameworks, and understood concepts of culture shock and even ethnography, I cannot recall ever learning that constructivism was used to explain these ideas and their origins. What Bennett offered was a much deeper conceptualization of culture than I had realized possible. Thus, in considering how constructivism might be useful in understanding intercultural communication, it may be useful to begin by defining culture.

---

[11] The reader should be aware that certain statements in this chapter are made for the purposes of illustrating the potential range of implications of constructivism and do not necessarily reflect the ultimate conclusions of this booklet.

Culture

Two of my favorite definitions of culture are "how people do their stuff together" and Bennett's more formal definition of subjective culture as "the learned and shared patterns of beliefs, behaviors, and values of groups of interacting people.[12]" Both of these definitions press beyond common conceptualizations of culture that limit it to the observable, as seen in:

1 | The food, music and style of dress of people in a foreign land;

2 | Fine arts such as a symphony or an opera;

3 | Stereotyped interactional style, such as the real or imagined differences between the ideas of "Minnesota Nice" and New York directness and

4 | Formalized patterns such as the social, economic, political, linguistic, and other such institutions.

Culture is an idea that certainly relates to all of these things, but as is indicated by the definitions above, the idea of culture that we will use describes a much more nuanced set of patterns.

If culture is the complex set of ways in which people determine answers to life's questions (doing their stuff together) - especially through the development of values, beliefs, and behaviors, then Crouch's definition of culture as "what we make of the world" is also helpful. From this perspective, anything that is human-made - a book, a car, a language, music, a political system, a philosophical system, an economy - all of these things could be considered to be elements of culture. Crouch's[13] approach also indicates a conceptual division between the world created by humans and the world created by God - the stars, our planet, the trees, our lives. The only non-created reality that we interact with is God Himself, and while we recognize that much of what we encounter in our daily lives was created by God, there is also sense in which much of what we experience in this world was "made" by us.

Radical Constructivism

Radical constructivists might suggest that Crouch's approach imposes an artificial division between the objective and subjective world. It is not so much that the objective world does not exist, but rather that the objective world is effectively inaccessible to humans,[14] because people necessarily experience the objective world subjectively.[15]

Radical constructivism thus suggests that it is appropriate to be skeptical when people suggest that they have found the

---

[12] Bennett, Basic *Concepts of Intercultural Communication,* 1998, 3.

[13] Crouch, *Culture Making.*

[14] von Glasersfeld, "An Introduction to Radical Constructivism.

[15] Singer, "Culture: A Perceptual Approach."

world as it really, objectively, truly is. The issue, according to radical constructivists is that proclamations of truth do not account for the situatedness of the speaker, who has learned how to think, how to perceive, and even what not to perceive.[16]

Whorf[17] and Kelly[18] suggest that the world is essentially experienced as meaningless (either as a "kaleidoscopic flux of impressions" or as "undifferentiated homogeneity") until people select, organize, evaluate stimuli from the world in the process of perception.[19] Importantly, the psychological need to understand the world is so intense that people will apply whatever frameworks they can to understand the world, even if such frameworks are actually poor fits to the world "as it really is".[20] Indeed, the process of knowing according to constructivists is the process of finding "truths" that fit the world rather than matching the world.[21] What people perceive then, is not the ultimate reality; rather "the environment as we perceive it is our invention."[22] If this is correct, then it means that there are actually many different and partially overlapping ways in which all the world could be interpreted.

---

[16] Singer; Kelly, *The Psychology of Personal Constructs*.

[17] Whorf, "Science and Linguistics."

[18] Kelly, *The Psychology of Personal Constructs*.

[19] Singer, "Culture: A Perceptual Approach."

[20] Kelly, *The Psychology of Personal Constructs*.

[21] Glasersfeld, "An Introduction to Radical Constructivism"; Glasersfeld, "Why People Dislike Radical Constructivism."

[22] Foerster, "On Constructing a Reality," 42.

Social Constructivism

While frameworks (constructs) are ultimately experienced individually,[23] many constructivists recognize the influence of social interaction on developing those frameworks, particularly through language, teaching, and reinforcement.[24] This understanding of the process of knowing suggests the need to understand what shapes the ways in which people come to construct the frameworks that they use to interpret the world.

The process of learning to interpret the world is shaped by social interactions in which knowledge is passed around, reinforced, and challenged.[25] It follows, then that the people who experience relatively similar processes and locations of socialization will tend to come to use similar frameworks to comprehend the world.[26] This does not, of course, mean that individuals will understand the world in exactly the same way or come to the same conclusions

---

[23] Ackermann, "Author's Response."

[24] Palmaru, "Making Sense and Meaning On the Role of Communication and Culture in the Reproduction of Social Systems"; Palmaru, "Author's Response"; Krippendorff, "Towards a Radically Social Constructivism"; Berger and Luckmann, The Social Construction of Reality; Kelly, The Psychology of Personal Constructs; Whorf, "Science and Linguistics."

[25] Berger and Luckmann, *The Social Construction of Reality*.

[26] Bennett, Basic Concepts of Intercultural Communication, 2013.

about the world.[27] But it does mean that they likely use the same or very similar underlying constructs to comprehend the world. These socialization groups will tend to share various characteristics because of the similarity of ways in which they comprehend the world, leading to the formation of culture, which "is constituted by the shared mental constructs of individuals."[28]

Social groups are comprised of individuals and individuals are members of social groups. This means that there is an ongoing back and forth and give and take between the individual and the group in shaping the understanding of the world. Radical constructivists tend to emphasize the role of the individual in shaping the group, while social constructivists tend to emphasize the role of the group in shaping the individual. However, it is probably most appropriate to understand both as influencing the other in an ongoing process.[29]

This process tends to be self-reinforcing, as "the institutions of culture are constantly re-created by people enacting their experience of those institutions."[30] However, the process of knowing does not result in a static set of knowledge, or in cultures which are fixed and unchanging. This leads to a brief consideration of how constructs are reinforced and changed. The approach used here is cybernetic constructivism.

---

[27] Singer, "Culture: A Perceptual Approach"; Kelly, *The Psychology of Personal Constructs*.

[28] Palmaru, "Author's Response," 69.

[29] Palmaru, "Author's Response."

[30] Bennett, *Basic Concepts of Intercultural Communication*, 2013, 7.

Cybernetic Constructivism

As knowledge is built by individuals in groups, people are constantly sending and receiving messages about how accurately each is understanding the other.[31] Sometimes variations will lead to changes for the individual, and sometimes they will challenge the construct held by the group. But for any of this to work, the senders and receivers of feedback messages must have ways to encode and decode those messages, and those sets of codes must correspond to one another.

This need for matching codes is one of the reasons that messages sent across cultural groups often do not result in the desired outcomes - messages encoded according to one set of codes are interpreted using a different set of codes. The more profound the difference between these codes, the less likely the message is to be understood as intended. However, even small differences in codes can cause major misunderstandings. If the message "I do not like that" is decoded as "I do like that", the interpretation is exactly wrong even though it is actually very close to being right.

A Summary of Constructivism

Social constructivism basically holds that much of the reality that we humans experience was created by people through social interactions. This idea of social constructivism relies on and gives rise to a number of related implications:

| **1** | *People's understanding of the world is necessarily shaped by their cultures, which are in turn shaped by people, in a constant and continuing process.* |

---

[31] Glasersfeld, "Knowledge for Sustainable Development."

| 2 | *Cultures make meaning largely through the use of symbols, especially as codified in their linguistic systems.* |

| 3 | *Both linguistic and cultural systems shape the ways in which people think to a very significant degree.* |

From here there are two main paths that can be taken:

| 1 | *Deterministic thinkers might suggest that it is not possible to think outside of the parameters offered by language and culture, as argued in the strong form of the Sapir-Whorf hypothesis.[32]* |

| 2 | *Others may prefer a more nuanced form of constructivism that suggests that language and culture influence the ways in which people think, but do not necessarily set determined limits to the possibilities of thought.* |

This second possibility seems more likely, but in either case, we are left with an understanding of the world that is largely human centered (anthropocentric) - humanity interacts with the world not merely as observers, but also as shapers of the meaning and experience of the world in an ongoing dialectical process. As we interact with the world around us, we develop linguistic explanations of that world (the human social world, the material/physical world, the spiritual world, etc.) and thus cause the creation of categories and ideas that may not have existed outside of our inventing them.

---

[32] Whorf, "Science and Linguistics."

By way of quick example, this is something like the problem of attempting to define the color "blue". What makes "blue" paint blue may indeed be the way that light waves interact with the pigment of that paint. However, the "blueness" of that paint is accorded by us, who gave it that label. Working out whether "blue for me is blue for you" again involves not reference to the work of the light interacting with the retina, but rather with what the brain does with that information.[33] We codify and give meaning to everything from shades of color (which we presume we experience in roughly similar ways) to the taste of coffee to highly complex human interactions. Consider as well the secondary meanings that we may give to these concepts - for example blue can stand for sadness, cool temperatures, and cleanliness in ways that may be inspired by the natural world, but which are certainly not required by the natural world.

As we humans have interacted with the world around us, we have adapted to it through the construction of frames that explain the world to us and allow us to interact with it. Some of these frames are adaptive and allow a society or culture to sustain itself while others are maladaptive and threaten the eventual survival of the group.[34]

It is important to recognize that even maladaptive frames serve explanatory purpose. For example, some would suggest that present American culture is maladaptive in as

---

[33] See Whorf for a variation on the question of blueness. Color-blindness introduces additional shades of meaning to these questions.

[34] Cohen, "A Theory and a Model of Social Change and Evolution."

much as it requires tremendous resource consumption, and that this is the case to such an extent that the processes by which these resources are accessed, or the byproducts of their use, will eventually yield an unsustainable situation in which the continuation of the American people (or of people generally) may be significantly threatened. That this pattern of resource consumption might ultimately threaten the culture does nothing to reduce the power of the understandings of the world that both necessitate and facilitate that resource consumption (including, for example, finding one's validation demonstrated through material gain). Of course, because constructivism involves a constant process, understandings currently held by the culture may change and (one might hope) yield less maladaptive and more adaptive constructions and patterns.

Assigning Values and the Trap of Reification

Once we explain phenomena using cultural constructions, we often then assign normative value to those phenomena (or at least to the constructions that interpret those phenomena to us), suggesting that some are good and some are bad. At times, according to committed constructivists, we forget that we have originally interpreted the world around us and made meaning, and we begin to interact with that meaning as though it were objectively there.[35] It is as though, for example, our conception of the color blue not only really exists as its own thing but perhaps even further that this color is inherently linked to the idea of sadness, as when one

---

[35] Bennett, "The Ravages of Reification: Considering the Iceberg and Cultural Intelligence, Towards de-Reifying Intercultural Competence."

"feels blue". When we forget that we have interpreted the world around us and assume that our own ideas have an a priori foundation, we have committed the constructivist sin of reification, by which we treat something as fundamentally and truly real even though it may be only as real as our perception of it. It may go like this: we have made something up, have forgotten we made it up, and then we proceed to make decisions that affect ourselves and others as though we were dealing with absolute truth.

Implications

There are many potential implications of a constructivist viewpoint. Four such implications are presented here. The reader who encounters discomfort with these four is encouraged to remember that some of that discomfort may be addressed in one of the following chapters of this booklet.

Ontological Options

If humanity understands the world through a process of (largely social) construction of reality, this may account in part for the many different ways in which people explain the origins and nature of the world, and of existence itself. This in turn has further implications in terms of the purpose of life and the way it "should" be lived. Intelligent Design and Evolution are but two of many constructed systems. Both of these systems are tied to explanations for why things exist in the first place. However, we should be suspicious if they claim to have discovered objective truth as it actually is. Such claims should be subject to scrutiny and potentially to some level of detachment. This level of uncertainty does not mean that there is not a first truth, or a first intelligent cause. However, constructivism draws attention to the questionability of our capacity to grasp that reality in a way that is fundamentally true to the first truth's essence.

Relativism

If all of humanity experiences reality through constructs created by humans, then no one cultural system has an inherent claim to deeper or truer knowledge than any other. Because of this, some suggest that morality can only be judged within cultural systems, but that it is inappropriate to judge morality across cultural systems, except perhaps where they find significant agreement. Normative statements of inherent goodness or badness may thus be highly questionable to the constructivist, because such evaluations are often based on reified, normative values. Constructivists may wrestle, for example, with the intersection between universal human rights on the one hand and cultural understandings of how humanity should live on the other hand.[36]

---

[36] This is, of course, a major challenge for advocates of universal human rights, and there is significant intellectual wrangling about these issues. Examples include: Bagish, "Confessions of a Former Cultural Relativist"; Donnelly, "Cultural Relativism and Universal Human Rights"; Cohen, "Human Rights and Cultural Relativism"; Bayefsky, "Cultural Sovereignty and Human Rights"; Zechenter, "In the Name of Culture"; Howard, "Are (should) Human Rights (be) Universal?"; de Varennes, "The Fallacies in the 'Universalism Versus Cultural Relativism' Debate in Human Rights Law"; Reichert, "Human Rights"; Donnelly, "The Relative Universality of Human Rights"; Donders, "Do Cultural Diversity and Human Rights Make a Good Match?"; Ng, "Are Human Rights a Western Construct?"; Oyowe, "An African Conception of Human Rights?"

Power and Society

Additionally, if all of humanity experiences reality by using constructs created by humans, then social, political, and other forms of power can be used to explain why some systems are more dominant than others. While there are also explanations available in terms of the eventual maladaptive or adaptive evaluation of a particular frame, the framework of power is very useful in exploring why it is that certain systems have gained and maintained influence. Critical theorists are particularly focused on exploring the ways that power is established and maintained in the socio-cultural context.[37]

The Necessity of Subjectivity

A further implication of social constructivism is that everything that a person perceives must be perceived subjectively. This does not necessarily deny the existence of objective reality or truth, but it does bring a serious challenge to humanity's grasp of the objective. This is as true in empirical science, which is sometimes praised as being a method intended to reveal the objective, as it is in art or religion - though it may be argued that even art and religion reflect elements of the objective, as well as of the subjective.

By way of example, I once challenged a professor of mine with the existence of bacteria - surely, I suggested, he could not dispute that bacteria caused disease. In a response that frustrated me at the time he responded that I was right, that bacteria do cause disease, or at least that

---

[37] Critical theorists trace their intellectual lineage to authors such as Adorno, Gramsci, Habermas, and Horkheimer, among others.

this was the case until we decide something different. In the few years since then, there has been a major popular expansion of the idea of probiotics, by which we have come to "know" that bacteria are a cause for health as well as for disease, and that the elimination of bacteria is by no means a guarantee of the absence of disease, and that the elimination of bacteria may even encourage the development of yet more potent bacteria. Yet we, in the United States at least, had reified the evils of bacteria to such an extent that our household cleaning products must claim to destroy bacteria in order for many Americans to feel comfortable buying them.

This was based on "scientific" knowledge that represented one of humanity's rigorous attempts at encountering the objective. Yet in this, and many other examples, we find that we cannot help but attach subjective meaning to the objective in our interpretation thereof. The question here is not whether the scientific evidence was incomplete, or the best of our knowledge at the time - there can be an expectation that future discoveries will disrupt current knowledge.

Instead, the issue is that the subjective experience is in fact our primary experience of scientific knowledge. Even what we believe we know objectively is still perceived by each person subjectively. I, for a time, perceived all bacteria as harmful and carried out my life as though this were true. Socially, I was marketed to as though it were true that all 'bacteria' were a thing to be feared and eradicated. Social knowing shaped my subjective experience of a complex objective reality that we are still learning more about. But that social knowing and subjective experience also caused me to act in a way that unnecessarily destroyed some bacteria, impacting the objective reality in which I live. Even though they are subjective, social constructs are not neutral.

Constructivism

Returning to the idea of subjective knowing, it seems not too far a stretch to suggest that humanity does, and each of us individually must, experience the world subjectively through the lenses given by our experiences and cultural ways of knowing. That the objective exists is not particularly contested (though of course it may be incredibly complicated[38]). Instead the assertion here is that in order for people to have a personal experience of even the most fundamental and objective realities, these must always be encountered and interpreted by each of us through necessarily subjective processes, which are in turn closely linked to social processes. Those processes may perhaps allow us to get near to expressing objective truth at times - but we nonetheless experience that objective truth subjectively.

---

[38] Hogenboom and Pirak, "Why There Could Be Many Identical Copies of You".

Social Constructivism and Christianity

Constructivism

Chapter Three
Common Christian Problems with Constructivism[39]

Having briefly considered social constructivism and the implications regarding ontological options, relativism, power, and subjectivity, we turn now to the two main Christian objections to constructivism. These are the existence of absolute truth and the problem of morality.[40]

---

[39] As with Chapter Two, the statements in this chapter should be understood as illustrative primarily of those views they intend to represent rather than as representing the ultimate conclusions of this booklet.

[40] The arguments in this chapter are based on my own interpretation of how Christians interact with these subjects, and it is likely that some will disagree with these assertions.

Absolute Truth

It is my observation that Christians who deny or at least limit social constructivism are often concerned that acceptance of constructivism requires the negation of absolute truth.

> **?** *If even the objective is perceived subjectively, then how do any of us know anything, and moreover, how would we know that we know it?*

This epistemological question is an important one, but rather than engaging it, some anti-constructivists stop there, assuming that this question has effectively dismissed the validity of constructivism.

Christians who reject constructivism on the grounds that it denies absolute truth have some merit in their concerns. Certainly constructivist approaches have been used by some to dismiss things that Christians believe are absolutely true - the existence of God is an important example.

There are, however, rather messier issues that some (especially Western) Christians have defended by appeal to absolute truth - these may include forms of morality, heterosexuality, the Holy Land, the process by which the world and the species came to be, and particularly for some American Christians, notions of freedom or liberty. While these items are still conflicted, it may serve as an appropriate warning to Christians today that some defenses of slavery were also founded on a variety of claims to absolute truth.[41]

---

[41] As explained by Emerson and Smith, *Divided by Faith*.

By diminishing the explanatory value of social constructivism, serious questions about these kinds of issues can be reduced or dismissed through an appeal to absolute truth. Christians who use the appeal to absolute truth may suggest that these are matters of faith, and that the faithful will submit themselves to the absolute truthfulness of these conclusions regardless of their personal, subjective experience of the topic.

Such an approach may have some biblical and theological merit, certainly at least enough that it is possible to validate such a position from certain hermeneutical perspectives. For example, the instruction to believe and not doubt (as in James 1:8) could be interpreted by some to suggest that doubts or questions about such issues are inappropriate and thus only the double-minded and unstable people ask such questions.

If one is faced with a choice between the relativistic experience and subjective interpretation of the world by the individual on the one hand and a claim of the necessity of submitting to absolute truth on the other, it is not surprising that some people, and in particular religious people, are far more comfortable with an appeal to absolute truth. Furthermore, if absolute truth claims happen to match many of such a person's pre-existing commitments this does not necessarily mean that such a person is in fact uncommitted to absolute truth, despite the apparent convenience of such a situation.[42]

---

[42] It is worth acknowledging that even among those who ardently defend absolute truth, there may be a tendency to make subjective claims about the absolute and absolute claims about the subjective.

Morality

The many different moral claims proffered by the many socio-cultural groups around the world have significant areas of overlap, tension, conflict, and irreconcilable difference between them.

Christian anti-constructivists reject the validity of moral relativism, by which a person should be judged according to the morals of his/her own cultural context. Such relativism seems to them suspiciously akin to the condition of the Hebrew people in the book of Judges (as in 17:6), when "everyone did what was right in their own eyes" - a condition the text indicates was not only undesirable, but wrong.

Those who distrust constructivism may do so because it seems to lead to a moral "slippery slope" in which each individual would eventually be free to do whatever they wish based on their socially constructed mores. Although there is at least some limitation to the accuracy of this argument,[43] there is also some truth in this, as observable major moral shifts that happen in societies over time. Such people may note that in numerous moral issues what was once unimaginable became imaginable; but it was still unthinkable. Even once it had become thinkable it was still unspeakable, and finally it became not only imaginable, thinkable, and speakable but normal. The progression of American attitudes around, and ultimately legalization of, same-sex marriage may be an example of this kind of change over time.

---

[43] Socially constructed mores cannot, by definition, be ultimately determined individually.

Turning Toward Synthesis

The concerns of the absolutist and the moralist are not here, I hope, trivialized. They are legitimate and serious contentions with very real effects on the human experience. However, as I hope to demonstrate in the following chapter, it is not necessary to address these by denigrating or dismissing the benefits of the social constructivist frame.

Common Christian Problems with Constructivism

Chapter Four
Relational Truth and Rational Truth

The goal of this chapter is to consider whether it is possible to apply social constructivism in an intellectually honest way and also affirm the core insights of a Christian worldview. One of the great challenges to doing this is the Western bias to the theologies that have dominated (Western) Christendom for the last thousand years, and in particular the dominance of white Europeans (and their descendants, including American Christians).[44]

The challenge is not particularly with the findings of white, Western theologians and biblical scholars. Instead, the challenge is that at least since the enlightenment Christian scholars from these backgrounds have tended

---

[44] Jenkins, The Lost History of Christianity; Escobar, The New Global Mission; Rah, The Next Evangelicalism; Twiss, Rescuing the Gospel from the Cowboys; Walls and Ross, Mission in the Twenty-First Century; Bradley, Aliens in the Promised Land.

to rely heavily on assumptions that are culturally limited without recognizing that this is the case.

My goal in this chapter is then to find an intellectually honest integration of social constructivism with a commitment to the core insights of Christian worldview. Although there are multiple ways to do this, I am looking to address a fundamental problem in accounting for different ways of knowing truth.

Namely this: It is necessary to discern a core truth that accounts not only for Western ways of knowing, but also for non-Western ways of knowing. This is critically important if Christianity is in fact a system that can be authentically contextualized into multiple different worldviews, which seems to be the case based on the work of the Lausanne organization, along with many contemporary missiologists.

How this Approach Connects to the Previous Chapters

Up to this point, this book has suggested several key points:

1. *Although a single objective reality may exist, it is never experienced directly by people. Instead, people experience the world through socially constructed ways of knowing. Thus, the world is always interpreted subjectively through constructs, rather than directly.*

2. *There are powerful implications to this initial observation, including:*

    a. *There is a range of ontological options or different ways in which existence can be explained.*

b	*Competing claims to truth share relative equality, in that they are all built through socially constructed interpretations of the world.*
c	*The distribution and exercise of power in society can be used to explain the privileging of certain truth claims over others.*
d	*Each person's experience of objective reality is necessarily subjective.*
3	*Christians who dislike or disagree with this understanding of reality may object to these ideas based upon concerns that constructivism threatens absolute truth and/or morality.*

The paragraphs that follow make an attempt to discern whether competing claims to truth, offered through two differently constructed systems, could in fact be connected to the same absolute reality, and whether the overlapping truths that they find could in fact point to a core truth - an approximation of absolute truth and of moral rootedness. Specifically, this is done through a consideration of the relation between truth and God.

Ways of Knowing:
An Oversimplified Introduction

The argument here is that if God can be known equally well (though differently) through multiple ways of knowing and yet still be fundamentally the same immutable (unchanging) God, then we must conceptualize a reality that can be both greater than all of those systems (a reality which we can call absolute truth, or Truth), and yet also knowable within them.

Imagine it this way. Both view A and view B have interpreted something about the world which is partially true and yet is incomplete. The question is whether the elements of truth that they represent can still be reconciled within a larger truth. Can view A of God and View B of God, both necessarily limited in and of themselves, be reconciled through a better understanding of the nature of God? Or must only one or the other (View A or View B) be correct? Or does the dissonance between them mean that there is no truth at all?

For our purposes (and in oversimplified terms) two main divisions of the ways in which God can be known are rational and relational knowing. These are briefly considered here as overgeneralized examples.[45]

---

[45] A much more developed discussion of similar concepts is available in Hiebert Transforming Worldviews.

This image, although far less complex than the natural world, contains many different patterns which people might attempt to turn into meaning. Several examples of meaning that people could attribute to the image are listed with a key at the end of the chapter. While many different "truths" can be isolated from this image, and while they can accurately reflect elements of the underlying truth, each is also limited to the extent that it does not encompass the totality of the image, including both at the large and small scale.

Rational Knowing

One of the popular ways of knowing has emphasized rational truth, in which human observers must verify any claim to truth through empirical verification. According to this view, nature can be divided into many disparate parts, each of which can be studied and examined separately. The division of natural organisms into classifications (i.e. genus and species) is a logical consequence of this approach. While it is itself a constructed way of knowing, the rationalist approach is very effective at generating certain kinds of knowledge.

The rationalist approach has been applied not only to the physical and natural sciences but also the social sciences. The study of human interactions as rational and predictable leans heavily upon the use of statistical analysis to identify patterns and to classify them as either significant or not significant.

In rational knowing, each truth proposition builds upon others in a linear fashion.

Those readers familiar with systematic theology may recognize the ways in which this approach to knowing has been applied to the study and interpretation of God and the bible in the Western context. To the Western theologian, God can be observed and understood (though perhaps within limits). Truth claims about God can be tested against other tested ideas about God, and no supposed truth can contradict any other previously determined truth about God.

Relational Knowing

There are many other ways of knowing, and just as our category of rational knowing is an oversimplification of several different epistemological systems, so relational knowing is an oversimplified approach to understanding several ways of knowing. However, enough of a core can be discerned for these to be treated together for the purpose of pursuing the present argument.

Relational knowing recognizes the human as existing within nature. Nature is indivisible and may be understood through the exploration of complex interconnected webs of causality. Intuitive and spiritual knowledge are not necessarily less valid, and may be considered as more valid, than observable or rational truths.

In relational knowing, connectedness truths - that is, truths that have more relational connections to the world known by the observer - have more validity than independently verifiable truths. Among other results, this means that disproving any particular element of a causal chain does not necessarily disprove the resultant "facts" of that chain, because there are other connected elements of reality that are supporting those ideas.

The treatment of miracles, for example, can be quite different from the rational and the relational frame. The rational knower may believe that it is possible to disprove a miracle through considering foundational preceding conditions. For example, if it can be proved that humans cannot walk on water through consideration of the surface tension of water, etc., then the story of Jesus' own walking on the water can be effectively discredited.

For the relational knower, on the other hand, proving that humans cannot walk on water does not necessarily have anything to do with whether Jesus (or even Peter) might have walked on water. The question is one of logic. For the rational knower, "A" (humans can walk on water) must precede "B" (Jesus walked on water). Without "A", "B" cannot happen. Rational thinkers looking to explain "B" must account for some quirk by which "A" could have happened in accordance to natural laws, which can, of course, lead to some bizarre explanations (i.e., he was standing on a fish's back).

However, the relational knower is under no such obligation to prove "A" in order for "B" to be true. That "A" is disproven - that is that humans cannot walk on water, does not necessarily pose a particular problem to "B" for the relational knower. There are so many other complex considerations in the interwoven and holistic web of reality that the relational knower may not be troubled at all to know how "B" happened in spite of "A", and either accepts it or rejects it based on other criteria. For example, the validity of the source (as in, who told the story) may be of far greater concern to the relational knower than is the propositional likelihood.

Constructivism and Knowing

The overly simplified treatments of these two ways of knowing presented above serve to illustrate one of the important points of social constructivism. Because people learn how to think within particular cultural contexts, it is difficult (though not necessarily impossible) for rational knowers to understand reality in the way that relational knowers understand it. The same is true in reverse.

So, if someone grows up in a culture which teaches them to know through rationality, it may be expected that if that person desires to know God, this will be accomplished primarily through rational means. Non-rational and subjective ways of knowing God may be considered dangerous and threatening to the knowable truths that such a person has discovered. Similarly, if someone is enculturated to knowing through relationality, then it may be expected that if that person desires to know God, this will be accomplished primarily through the holistic, non-divisive ways of knowing familiar to such a person. Rational ways of knowing God may be considered threatening or pointless (why divide the indivisible?).

Constructivism allows us to see that both the rational approach and the relational approach are socially constructed ways of knowing. Both rational and relational thinkers may believe in absolutes, though they are likely to be conceptualized and experienced quite differently.

I argue here that if it is possible to know the absolute, then we may expect it to be both greater than, and accessible within, both rational and relational ways of knowing. That is, the fundamental truth of the world should be able to be known by both "view A" and "view B".

Fundamental Truth

How then can that fundamental truth - the First Cause and Holistic Truth - be knowable both within rational and relational ways of knowing?

The core argument of this short book is that the First Cause and Holistic Truth is best understood as being the particular person of the God of the Bible, known to us today as YHWH, Jesus, and the Holy Spirit[46]. I hold that truth is fundamentally a Person, and that Person is the Answer beyond which there are no further answers. The fundamental Truth of the universe is the Word who was with God and is God in John 1:1.

Let us first test the argument against the rational and relational socially constructed ways of knowing, and then consider several implications of this argument.

---

[46] Naturally, language is limited in describing the personhood of the Ultimate, and it is common to refer to the 3 in 1 as the Trinity. The complexities of the 3 in 1 are not a core issue of this work and thus further consideration of the word is omitted from the major text.

Knowing Truth Differently

If it is agreed that Truth is infinite and because humanity is finite, we are not surprised to see that different groups of humanity have interpreted that truth differently, even to the extent of interpreting the nature of truth and the nature of knowing differently. This is not surprising - much as each of our different friends has a unique relationship with us, or as children each have a unique relationship with their parent. So it is with humanity, through human culture, and the Person who is Absolute. That we are interacting with that truth through different epistemological understandings does not mean that it is necessarily true or untrue, though the existence of the interaction from multiple perspectives may help triangulate the nature and character of Truth. However, as with a parent and children, interaction alone does not always mean that there is a healthy relationship in which both are accurately understood by each other. I argue that both the relational and the rational knower are potentially satisfied through the understanding of Truth as a person, without fundamental conflict between them.

Relational

It is at first perhaps easier to see the connection between relational knowing and the concept of Truth as a person. Knowledge is discoverable within the holistic understanding of who Truth is, and it is expected that there is a great deal of complexity within this understanding. Moreover, as the relational thinker expects, Truth is ultimately indivisible. Harmony with and submission to the ultimate One are appropriate goals. Moreover, the Christian gospel reveals that Truth Himself has provided a method for achieving this harmony at His own cost through the sacrifice of Jesus.

Rational

Rational thinkers are not, however, left wanting. Indeed, if Truth is a person, then to the extent that we know that person we are able to accurately understand everything that is. I suggest that causality exists within a framework for being that Truth has authored. Moreover, because Truth is immutable, it is both possible and appropriate to look for consistency within the world that Truth has authored. The trouble for rational thinkers is that the construction of rationality tends to look fundamentally for a non-organic, non-relational first cause. If this tendency is replaced with a recognition that the first cause is a Person (as in, the Person of Christ), propositional logic works better than without this First Cause.

Implications

If this assertion regarding truth (that Truth is fundamentally a Person) can be understood both within rational and relational epistemological systems then constructivism does not necessarily need to be understood as a threat to Truth. Rather the opposite - as mentioned above, the opportunity for triangulation may allow for a closer and more accurate understanding of Truth's person and character. Moreover, the concerns of the absolutist and moralist can be addressed - though perhaps not in the way they would prefer, in a way that is nonetheless satisfactory in answering the problems posed.

The Absolutist and Moralist and Truth

This idea of Truth revealing Himself to humanity is found all through the Bible, both in the Old and New Testaments. Genesis sets the stage of Truth's interaction with people. Exodus explains the journey of a particular people in being rescued by and coming to know Truth. Through the rest of the Old Testament that people bears witness to human limitations in being accountable to the Truth they have encountered and yet Truth presses on, revealing more and more about reality, including through the chastisement of His people, through the prophets, and through the exile and return.

The New Testament reveals even more about who Truth is, as Truth incarnate lives among humanity and reveals the character of Truth in the flesh. Truth sacrifices Himself and yet returns to life so that humanity can be reconciled with Truth. And, like in the Old Testament, Truth appoints a New Testament people to bear witness to the nature of Truth.

Admittedly, both the Old Testament and New Testament people of God have struggled mightily to represent the character of Truth accurately. However, this points to the limitations of humanity in knowing and living truth accurately, which is very much in keeping with the theme of this book.

Those who have never encountered the Old or New Testament have nonetheless encountered much about Truth. Romans 1 and 2 explains that both nature itself (the world, the universe) and human nature (the law "written on our hearts") reveal much about the character of Truth. Thus both through general revelation (nature and human nature- [Romans chapters 1 and 2]) and through special revelation (the Bible, Jesus incarnate, and the Holy Spirit), humanity has encountered Truth.

That people are finite and that there are different ways to interpret these revelations of Truth to humanity in no way invalidates the claim that Truth has nonetheless revealed Himself and that humanity is morally responsible for living consistently with the Truth that has been revealed.

Thus, the absolutist is correct in suggesting that absolute truth exists. A Christian constructivist need not reject the concept of absolute truth. Indeed, much about Truth is indeed knowable. However, both the absolutist and the constructivist should be humble about the accuracy and extent to which they have grasped Truth. The absolutist bears witness to the reality that Truth exists. The constructivist bears witness to the reality that every human attempt at knowing truth and Truth is limited by human subjectivity and that our experience of truth and Truth are necessarily filtered through social constructions.

The moralist is also correct in suggesting that righteous living matters. As has been discussed, there are things that humans know about the character of Truth to which people are indeed accountable. A Christian constructivist need not reject the concept of universally applicable moral standards. The constructivist contributes a powerful insight, however: moral understanding is always filtered through subjectively experienced social constructs. Each of those constructs is an approximation of truth rather than exact fit to it. Thus both moral fervor and humility are warranted - not separately, but together. Paul addresses an issue in the early church suggesting that it was appropriate to "let each one be thoroughly convinced in his own mind" (Rom 14:5). However, Paul also makes it clear that this freedom of interpretation did not lead to total moral freedom (Romans 2:4, 6:15). Instead, the love of one another was to govern the exercise of moral freedom, because that love was rooted in and reflected the character of the person of Truth (Galatians 5:13-14).

Where Do We Go from Here?

The argument of this chapter has built on the previous chapters by suggesting that Truth is fundamentally a person, and that this Person, and the Truth, can be known both through rationally and relationally constructed ways of knowing. This led to both affirmations and rebukes to the absolutist and moralist objections to constructivism. Both are partly correct, but they are also shortsighted if they believe they have grasped Truth directly, without the use of social constructs. However, the constructivist need not, and the Christian constructivist ought not, reject truth nor morality.

This is really important to recognize. A student once suggested that Christian constructivists are scary because they can choose whatever truth suits them best for a particular moment or situation. However, this ought not to be the case. A Christian constructivist - whether epistemologically rational or relational (or something else) - ideally recognizes that while multiple constructs may fit a particular situation, they must always be selected and employed with reference to the character of the Person who is Truth. There is much freedom here, but there is also a strong anchor.

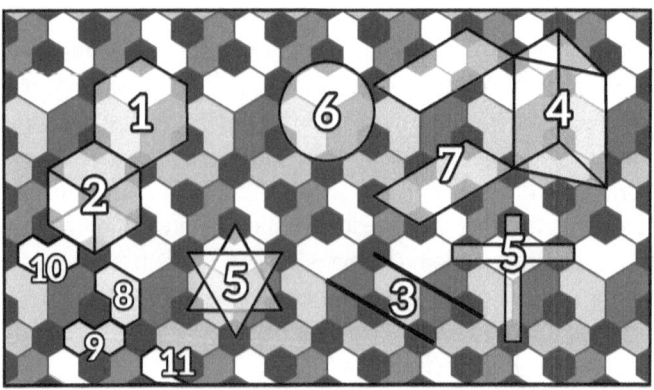

1	*The absence of a central dot within the hexagonal array of black dots in this line, as contrasted with the line below;*
2a	*The outside bottom of a grey box;*
2b	*The outside top of a grey box;*
2c	*The inside bottom of a grey box;*
3	*The presence of parallel lines that continue throughout the image, though occasionally hidden from view;*
4	*The emergence of 3D superstructures such as this wedge;*
5	*The inclusion of religious symbols, such as this cross and star of David;*
6	*The inclusion of overlapping circles, which each borrow points from other circles;*
7	*parallel planes. Additionally, the black hexagons could either be perceived as something added in front of the underlying image, or as the base image, in front of which another image (which has hexagon shaped holes) has been placed. If the black hexagons and the black lines are seen this way, then we are left with several very strange shapes like 8, 9, 10, and 11, while the black hexagons and lines represent the absence of something, rather than a something.*
10	*Interestingly, shape 10 also resembles a heart.*

Different meanings can be isolated from this image - none are complete without the others, even though they all seem in some ways to be competing. However that does not mean truth is a free-for all. Despite all of the many meanings that may be contained here, it would still be false to claim that this image is colored red, orange, yellow, green, blue, indigo, or violet (assuming it is printed with black ink).

Relational Truth and Rational Truth

Conclusion

The goal of this short book is to make the constructivist approach available to Christians. There are many follow-up questions that can be considered. Can constructs be chosen? Can meaning be exchanged between people who understand Truth through different epistemological constructs?

Beyond these questions, there are applications of various forms of constructivism to the many different fields in which it is applied. In intercultural relations, international relations, mathematics, education, and beyond, many different constructivisms can be found. It is hoped that this book has laid enough a foundation that those who desire to move forward have encountered enough initial resources to do so.

Resources

As the reader will no doubt recognize, this booklet has only scratched the surface of several different and very complicated areas of thought and study. Recognizing the necessarily limited depth of this writing, I strongly encourage you, the reader to further pursue these questions through reference to following resources. Readers new to these concepts may find that reading them in the order listed below is helpful.

Intercultural Communication: A Current Perspective: Milton J. Bennett

A Constructivist Frame for Intercultural Communication: Milton J. Bennett

The Myth of Certainty: Daniel Taylor

The Social Construction of Reality: Berger and Luckman

Culture: A Perceptual Approach: Marshall R. Singer (available in Bennett)

Science and Linguistics: Benjamin Lee Whorf (available in Bennett)

Intercultural Epistemology and Paradigmatic Confusion: Milton J. Bennett

Works Cited

Ackermann, E. K. "Author's Response: Impenetrable Minds, Delusion of Shared Experience: Let's Pretend ('dicciamo Che Io Ero La Mamma')." *Constructivist Foundations* 10, no. 3 (2015): 418-21.

Bagish, Henry H. "Confessions of a Former Cultural Relativist." Santa Barbara City College Publications, 1981. http://frc.sbcc.edu/4sbccfaculty/lecture/80s/lectures/Henry_Bagish_print.html.

Bayefsky, Anne F. "Cultural Sovereignty, Relativism, and International Human Rights: New Excuses for Old Strategies." *Ratio Juris* 9, no. 1 (March 1996): 42-59.

Bennett, Milton J. *Basic Concepts of Intercultural Communication: Paradigms, Principles, & Practice: Selected Readings*. Second Edition. Boston: Intercultural Press, A Nicholas Brealey Pub. Company, 2013.

———. *Basic Concepts of Intercultural Communication: Selected Readings*. Nicholas Brealey Publishing, 1998.

———. "The Ravages of Reification: Considering the Iceberg and Cultural Intelligence, Towards de-Reifying Intercultural Competence." Colle Val d'Elsa,

Italy: Intercultural Development Research Institute, 2013. http://www.idrinstitute.org/allegati/IDRI_t_Pubblicazioni/77/FILE_Documento_Intercultura_Reification.pdf.

Berger, Peter L., and Thomas Luckmann. *The Social Construction of Reality: A Treatise in the Sociology of Knowledge*. Anchor, 1967.

Bradley, Anthony B. *Aliens in the Promised Land: Why Minority Leadership Is Overlooked in White Christian Churches and Institutions*. Phillipsburg, New Jersey: P & R Pub, 2013.

Cohen, Ronald. "Human Rights and Cultural Relativism: The Need for a New Approach." *American Anthropologist* 91, no. 4 (1989): 1014-17.

Cohen, Yehudi A. "A Theory and a Model of Social Change and Evolution." *Journal of Anthropological Archaeology* 2, no. 2 (June 1, 1983): 164-207. https://doi.org/10.1016/0278-4165(83)90011-9.

Crouch, Andy. *Culture Making: Recovering Our Creative Calling*. Intervarsity Press, 2008.

Donders, Yvonne. "Do Cultural Diversity and Human Rights Make a Good Match?" *International Social Science Journal* 61, no. 199 (March 1, 2010): 15-35. https://doi.org/10.1111/j.1468-2451.2010.01746.x.

Donnelly, Jack. "Cultural Relativism and Universal Human Rights." *Human Rights Quarterly* 6, no. 4 (1984): 400-419. https://doi.org/10.2307/762182.

———. "The Relative Universality of Human Rights." *Human Rights Quarterly* 29, no. 2 (2007): 281-306

Emerson, Michael O., and Christian Smith. *Divided by*

Faith: *Evangelical Religion and the Problem of Race in America*. Oxford University Press, USA, 2001.

Escobar, Samuel. *The New Global Mission: The Gospel from Everywhere to Everyone*. IVP Academic, 2003.

Foerster, Heinz von. "On Constructing a Reality." *In The Invented Reality: How Do We Know What We Believe We Know? (Contributions to Constructivism)*, edited by Paul Watzlawick, 1 edition., 41-61. New York: W W Norton & Co Inc, 1984.

Glasersfeld, Ernst von. "An Introduction to Radical Constructivism." *In The Invented Reality: How Do We Know What We Believe We Know? (Contributions to Constructivism)*, edited by Paul Watzlawick, 1 edition., 17-40. New York: W W Norton & Co Inc, 1984.

———. "Cybernetics and the Theory of Knowledge." *Knowledge for Sustainable Development: An Insight into the Encyclopedia of Life Support Systems*. Paris: UNESCO/EOLSS, 2002. http://www.vonglasersfeld.com/255.

———. "Why People Dislike Radical Constructivism." *Constructivist Foundations* 6, no. 1 (2010): 19-21. Hiebert, Paul G. *Transforming Worldviews: An Anthropological Understanding of How People Change*. Grand Rapids, Mich: Baker Academic, 2008.

Hogenboom, Meliss, and Pierangelo Pirak. *Why There Could Be Many Identical Copies of You*. BBC Earth, 2016. http://www.bbc.com/earth/story/20161021-why-there-could-be-many-copies-of-you.

Howard, Rhoda E. "Are (should) Human Rights (be) Universal?" *Update on Law-Related Education*. 22, no. 3 (October 15, 1998): 29-32.

Jenkins, John Philip. *The Lost History of Christianity: The Thousand-Year Golden Age of the Church in the Middle East, Africa, and Asia--and How It Died*. First Edition first Printing. HarperOne, 2008.

Kelly, George A. *The Psychology of Personal Constructs*. 1. publ. in Norton paperback 1963. Vol. 1: A Theory of Personality. New York: Norton, 1963.

Krippendorff, K. "Towards a Radically Social Constructivism." *Constructivist Foundations 3*, no. 2 (2008): 91-94.

Meer, Nasar, Tariq Modood, and Ricard Zapata-Barrero, eds. *Multiculturalism and Interculturalism: Debating the Dividing Lines*. Edinburgh: Edinburgh University Press, 2016.

Ng, Thomas. "Are Human Rights a Western Construct? From the Confucius Peace Prize to the Practice of Suttee in India." *Journal of International Social Research* 5, no. 21 (Spring 2012): 465-67.

Oyowe, Oritsegbubemi. "An African Conception of Human Rights? Comments on the Challenges of Relativism." *Human Rights Review* 15, no. 3 (September 2014): 329-47. https://doi.org/10.1007/s12142-013-0302-2.

Palmaru, Raivo. "Author's Response: Culture Matters." *Constructivist Foundations* 8, no. 1 (November 2012): 80-84.

———. "Making Sense and Meaning On the Role of Communication and Culture in the Reproduction of Social Systems." *Constructivist Foundations* 8, no. 1 (November 2012): 63-75.

Rah, Soong-Chan. *The Next Evangelicalism: Freeing the*

Church from Western Cultural Captivity. IVP Books, 2009. Reichert, Elisabeth. "Human Rights: An Examination of Universalism and Cultural Relativism." *Journal of Comparative Social Welfare* 22, no. 1 (April 2006): 23-36. https://doi.org/10.1080/17486830500522997.

Riegler, A. "Editorial. The Constructivist Challenge." *Constructivist Foundations* 1, no. 1 (2005): 1-8

Singer, Marshall R. "Culture: A Perceptual Approach." *In Basic Concepts of Intercultural Communication: Selected Readings*, edited by Milton J. Bennett, 97-109. Nicholas Brealey Publishing, 1998.

Twiss, Richard. Rescuing the Gospel from the Cowboys: *A Native American Expression of the Jesus Way*. Downers Grove: InterVarsity Press, 2015.

Varennes, Fernand de. "The Fallacies in the 'Universalism Versus Cultural Relativism' Debate in Human Rights Law." *Asia-Pacific Journal on Human Rights & the Law* 7, no. 1 (January 2006): 67-84. https://doi.org/10.1163/157181506778218120.

Walls, Andrew F., and Cathy Ross, eds. *Mission in the Twenty-First Century: Exploring the Five Marks of Global Mission*. Maryknoll, N.Y: Orbis Books, 2008.

Whorf, Benjamin L. "Science and Linguistics." *In Basic Concepts of Intercultural Communication: Selected Readings*, edited by Milton J. Bennett, 85-95. Nicholas Brealey Publishing, 1998.

Zechenter, Elizabeth M. "In the Name of Culture: Cultural Relativism and the Abuse of the Individual." *Journal of Anthropological Research* 53, no. 3 (1997): 319-47.

About the author

Stephen W. Jones is Assistant Professor of International Studies at Crown College in St. Bonifacius, MN. He is in the process of earning his Ph.D. in International Development from the University of Southern Mississippi and holds a Master of Arts in Intercultural Relations from the University of the Pacific (Stockton, CA) in conjunction with the Intercultural Communication Institute (Portland, OR). He also has a B.A. in Bible and Intercultural Studies and a B.S. in Business Administration: Intercultural Management from Grace University (Omaha, NE).

Jones's introduction to teaching in the field of intercultural studies came when he delivered an intensive Cultural Anthropology course for an American university in Mali, West Africa in 2007. He has worked with groups involved in overseas study and service in Africa, Europe, Latin America, and Asia, as well as in various subcultures of the United States. Jones has rich personal experience in various cultural settings and in industries ranging from agriculture to hospitality to higher education to financial services. Jones is also the author of "Transitions Across Cultures".

To find out more, find us at www.iamintercultural.com.

www.ingramcontent.com/pod-product-compliance
Lightning Source LLC
Chambersburg PA
CBHW030131100526
44591CB00009B/612